Top 30 Moringa Tree FAQ

Questions and Answers!

By Rene' and Cornelius Epps II

1. Q: What is the Moringa Oleifera main purpose?

A: It is to; detox the Liver of any toxins allowing this work-horse of all organs to distribute the proper nutrition to the body which causes a chain of positive events to occur.

2. Q: What is Moringa?

A: Moringa is a healing medicinal tree that has been used for hundreds of years by cultures of the world such as Africa, Asia, and India. Moringa has 7X more Vitamin C than Oranges
4X more Vitamin A than Carrots
4X more Calcium & 2X more protein than Milk
3X more Potassium than Bananas
3X more Iron than Almonds
*Moringa has 40% protein per serving, contains all 8 essential amino acids (18 aminos total). Contains over 40 antioxidants, including flavonoids. Moringa is said to cure and/or prevent over 300 ailments.

3. Q: Storing Moringa Seeds?

Our seeds are fresh; in good condition, you can store seeds in a paper bag or zip lock bag, keep them dry, because if they get wet, 'they' ll sprout'. <u>**Do NOT Freeze or Refrigerate,**</u> keep away from any cold areas, they will die. 60-80 degrees is a good temperature to store them. They can last a few years; though the germination rate may drop the older they get.

4. Q: Storing Moringa leaf powder?

A: You can store the powder as you would dried herbs, or spices; in a bag, or a jar, keeping it in a dry place.

5. Q: Is Moringa An Herb?

A: No Moringa is not an herb. It is a super-food; more like a vegetable that has basically everything in it, needed, to sustain life in general. Not like many herbs that may have some side affects and cannot be used when pregnant or nursing.

Moringa can be eaten anytime while pregnant, and or breast-feeding. It is also given to babies and is very helpful with reproduction in the male genitalia.

6. Q: How to eat Moringa?

A: You can eat moringa leaves raw; juice them, fry, or steam them in any meal. Bake moringa in cookies, drink as a tea, dry the leaves for powder, and add to shakes or smoothies.

7. Q: Can I eat Moringa roots?

A: Some cultures eat the roots, but we don't recommend eating the roots. The root bark has Neurotoxin in it, which may be fatal *in high dosages.*

8. Q: How does Moringa taste?

A: It taste like mild spinach and becomes

sweeter when cooked.

9. Q: Does Moringa stenopetala have the same

health benefits as Moringa oleifera?

A: Yes they both have all the same health

benefits. Though they may differ

in percentage slightly.

10. Q: Can I grow a Moringa tree where I live?

A: You can grow Moringa anywhere with care. Cold climates you can grow them in large pots. Warm climates they grow great in the ground, year around.

11. Q: How to Grow Moringa trees in potted containers?

Plant seeds in a small pot first; then Transplant gradually from 1-5 gallons. Just remember, the larger the pot, the bigger the tree will grow.

12. Q: Does Moringa Trees grow fast?

A: Moringa Oleifera grow very fast; up to 20+ feet in one year, if the temperature stays warm and hot year around.

Moringa stenopetalas grow slower and can die easier in the cold. If either tree dies back in the winter, most of the time, they'll grow back come spring time.

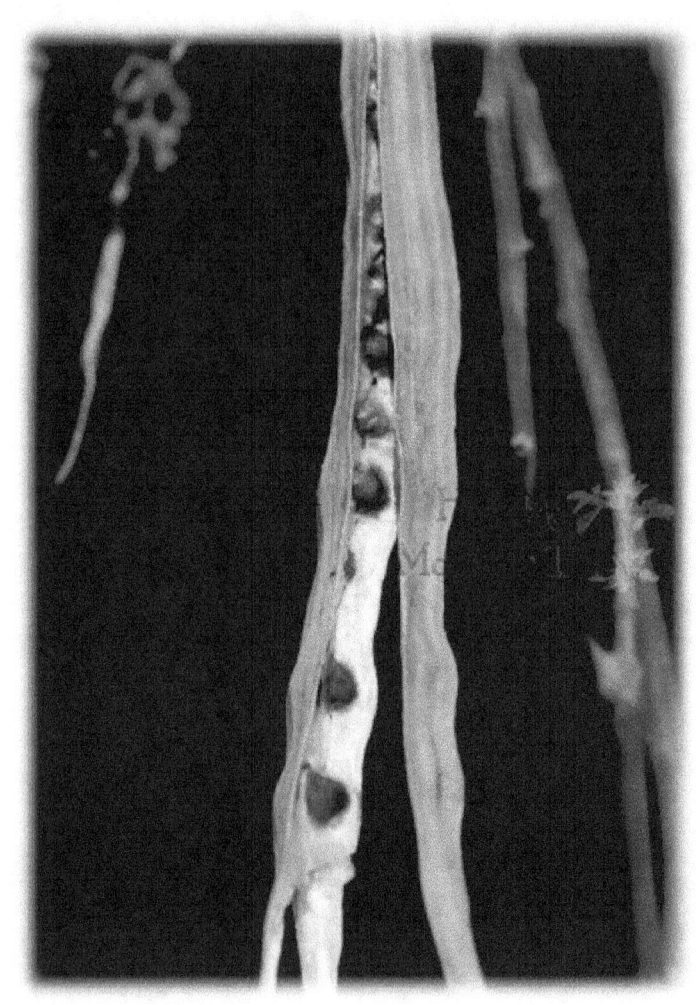

13. Q: When does the Moringa produce seedpods?

A: Moringa Oleifera takes 6-18 months for seed pod production depending on location. Moringa Stenopetala takes 2+ years for seed pod production. Other Moringa species take 4+ years for seeds.

14. Q: What do Moringa pods taste like?

A: They taste somewhat like peanuts. Moringa pods are highly nutritious and contain the essential amino acids and vitamins our body needs.

15. Q: How often should I water a Moringa tree?

A: Depending on weather and climate. Humid areas need less water than hotter dry places. We water once or twice a day, only when plants are 5 inches, to 3 feet tall. Only when they get woody barks do they become drought tolerant plants and don't require as much water.

16. Q: Why do Moringa tree leaves change yellow?

A: There may be more than one cause. Not enough water; Moringas are a tropical tree and love water. Yellow leaves can be the result of too much water around the roots, or if the soil is too clay-like, "compacted",

which can result in root rot very quickly.
In very hot and dry areas young Moringa
leaves will yellow without enough water,
especially in pots when the soil gets very dry.
Moringa Fungal disease; this fungus takes over
plants slowly making the leaves yellow with
small brown spots until killing it. Pest on
Moringa trees may also cause yellowing.

17. Q: What about Gamma irradiation in Moringa?

A: This is a sterilization process where products are exposed to gamma rays, a form of electromagnetic radiation which kill and destroys bacteria and pathogens. This process should be avoided with Moringa leaves, which causes nutritional value loss.

18. Q: When can I harvest and eat Moringa leaves?

A: It is best to harvest Moringa leaves when the trees are about 3 feet tall.

Moringa Stenopetala Seedling

19. Q: Is Moringa leaf tea more beneficial than consuming the Moringa leaves.

A: Although the tea may have similar benefits, it's always best to actually consume the leaves of the Moringa plant for the complete benefit.

20. Q: What is a Moringa tree necessity?

A: Sunlight and warmth, they will not survive without it.

21. Q: When is a Moringa tree drought tolerant?

A: Moringa trees are drought tolerant when they get woody barks, after about one year.

22. Q: I transplanted my Moringa, now it's drooping?

A: If you Transplant your Moringa and it starts to droop, wait for about 7-14 days, sometimes they might start to die, then the roots will catch. When this happens, look for new branches at the top and at the base. Within a few days they should show.

23. Q: How do I prune my Moringa tree?

A: Always prune from the top, and cut branches halfway for better stimulation.

24. Q: Why Prune a Moringa Tree?

A: A Moringa can become very tall and get out of reach if not pruned. Also, pruning makes them become more abundant with leaves than if not pruned.

25. Q: What are some other Moringa tree names around the world?

A: Ben Oil Tree, Malunggay, Wasabi, Moonga, Murunga, Sojina, Murungai Maram, Chum Ngay, Dangap, Malugkai, Sahjan, Brède Mouroum, Saragvo, Kelor, Shobhanjana, horse radish, cabbage tree, drum stick tree.

26. Q: How can one tell pure Moringa seed oil?

A: Good Question, because everyone sells Moringa oil online right?

One-way to tell if the oil is pure Moringa seed oil, put it in a refrigerator, and if the oil becomes cloudy, or hardens, most likely it's pure. If it stays liquid most likely, it has been blended with some other oils.

Moringa Stenopetala

27. Q: How many antioxidants does Moringa have?

A: There are more than 46 antioxidants in Moringa Oleifera

28. Q: Is Moringa oleifera a superfood?

Yes it is, because it's loaded with high amounts of vitamins, protein, and amino acids that are essential to life.

29. Q: Can I lose weight with Moringa?

A: Moringa has been known to help increase weight loss due to its liver detoxification properties.

There are many success stories of weight loss with the use of Moringa.

Moringa Drouhardii Seedling

30. Q: How many Moringa Tree Species are there?

A: There are about 13 species of Moringa trees in the Moringaceae family. Native to Africa, Middle east and India.

Order our 2 books special

How to grow a Moringa Tree!

www.HealingMoringaTree.com